WILDFIRES

BOOK FOR SMART KIDS

Learn About the Causes, Prevention, and Impact of Wildfires and What You Can Do to Help

MARTY HODGEF

TABLE OF CONTENTS

INTRODUCTION

Wildfires are one of the most destructive natural disasters on Earth. They can start quickly, spread rapidly, and cause extensive damage to ecosystems, homes, and infrastructure. Every year, wildfires affect millions of acres of land and impact the lives of countless people and animals.

Despite their destructive power, wildfires are a natural part of many ecosystems, and they play an important role in maintaining the health of forests, grasslands, and other landscapes. In fact, some plants and animals have evolved to rely on wildfires to regenerate and thrive.

Understanding wildfires is critical for both our safety and the health of the environment. Wildfires can have devastating effects on the air we breathe, the water we drink, and the habitats of animals that call these areas home. In addition, wildfires can be incredibly dangerous for people who live in or near affected areas, as they can spread quickly and be difficult to control.

However, wildfires are not always bad. In fact, some fires are necessary to help ecosystems maintain a healthy balance. For example, certain trees and plants require fire to release their seeds and promote new growth. Wildfires can also help clear out dead or diseased plants, making room for new growth and helping to prevent the spread of pests and diseases.

In this book, we will explore the science of wildfires, their causes, and effects, how they are prevented and fought, and what happens in the aftermath of a wildfire. We will also provide tips for staying safe during wildfire season and explain why it is so important for everyone to do their part in preventing wildfires.

Whether you live in an area prone to wildfires or just want to learn more about these fascinating and powerful natural phenomena, this book is for you. We hope that by the end of this book, you will have a deeper understanding of wildfires and their impact on the world around us and be better prepared to stay safe and protect our planet. So let's dive in and learn about wildfires!

CHAPTER 1:

What Causes Wildfires?

Wildfires can be caused by both natural and human factors. Understanding these causes is an important step in preventing and managing wildfires.

1. Natural Causes of Wildfires

- **Lightning:**

Lightning strikes are a common natural cause of wildfires. In fact, lightning is responsible for starting around 10% of all wildfires in the United States.

- **Heat:**

High temperatures and dry conditions can cause wildfires to start naturally. In California, for example, a single heat wave in 2020 led to more than 650 wildfires.

- **Volcanic eruptions:**

Although relatively rare, volcanic eruptions can cause wildfires. The 1980 eruption of Mount St. Helens, for example, led to a wildfire that burned more than 150 square miles of forest.

2. Human Causes of Wildfires

- **Campfires:**

Campfires are a common human cause of wildfires. In fact, campfires are responsible for starting around 85% of all wildfires caused by humans in the United States.

- **Smoking:**

Discarding cigarette butts improperly can also start wildfires. It's estimated that cigarette butts are responsible for starting around 4% of all wildfires in the United States.

- **Sparks from equipment:**

Sparks from equipment like lawnmowers, power tools, and vehicles can also ignite wildfires if they come into contact with dry vegetation or other combustible materials. In California, for example, equipment use is responsible for around 5% of all wildfires caused by humans.

- **Arson:**

Sadly, some wildfires are caused by intentional acts of arson. In the United States, arson is responsible for starting around 1% of all wildfires.

It's important to note that humans are responsible for the vast majority of wildfires. In fact, it's estimated that up to 90% of wildfires are caused by humans.

Understanding the causes of wildfires is important, but it's just as important to take steps to prevent them. Some ways to prevent wildfires include properly extinguishing campfires, disposing of cigarettes properly, and being cautious with equipment that can create sparks. It's also important to follow local laws and regulations regarding fire safety and to be aware of any wildfire warnings or alerts in your area.

In the next chapter, we'll dive deeper into the science of wildfires, exploring how they start and spread, as well as different types of wildfires and the role of weather in wildfire behavior.

CHAPTER 2:

The Science of Wildfires

Wildfires are complex and dynamic phenomena, and understanding the science behind them is important for preventing and managing them.

1. How Wildfires Start

- **Ignition:**

Wildfires start when a spark or heat source ignites the fuel, which can be anything from dry grass to dead trees. Once ignited, the fire can quickly spread if the conditions are right.

- **Fuel:**

The fuel for a wildfire is the vegetation and other materials that the fire burns. The type of fuel, as well as its quantity and moisture content, can all affect how a wildfire behaves.

2. How Wildfires Spread

- **Convection:**

Convection is the process by which heat rises and draws in more air, which can feed the fire and cause it to spread. This is why wildfires can create their own weather patterns, including thunderstorms and strong winds.

- **Radiation:**

Radiation is another way that wildfires can spread. As the fire burns, it radiates heat in all directions, which can ignite nearby fuel and cause the fire to spread.

- **Conduction:**

Conduction occurs when heat is transferred directly from one object to another. In the case of wildfires, conduction can cause the fire to spread from tree to tree, for example.

3. Types of Wildfires

- **Surface fires:**

Surface fires burn only the surface layer of vegetation and do not usually cause significant damage to trees or soil.

- ## **Crown fires:**

Crown fires burn through the tops of trees and can be much more destructive than surface fires.

- ## **Ground fires:**

Ground fires burn through the organic material in the soil and can be difficult to control.

4. The Role of Weather

- ## **Temperature:**

High temperatures can dry out vegetation and make it more susceptible to ignition.

- ## **Humidity:**

Low humidity can make vegetation more flammable and contribute to the spread of wildfires.

- **Wind:**

Strong winds can spread wildfires more quickly and make them more difficult to control.

It's important to note that while wildfires can be devastating, they also play an important ecological role. For example, many plant species have evolved to depend on periodic wildfires for their survival, and wildfires can also help to control invasive species and promote biodiversity.

However, it's also important to take steps to prevent and manage wildfires, including following fire safety regulations, being cautious with fire and equipment that can create sparks, and staying informed about wildfire warnings and alerts in your area.

In the next chapter, we'll explore the impacts of wildfires on people, wildlife, and the environment, as well as the strategies used to manage and fight wildfires.

CHAPTER 3:

The Effects of Wildfires

Wildfires can cause devastating effects on the environment, wildlife, and people. The effects of wildfires can be both immediate and long-term.

1. Immediate Effects

- **Destruction:**

Wildfires can destroy homes, buildings, and other infrastructure. They can also burn through entire forests, grasslands, and other ecosystems. For example, in 2020, wildfires burned over 10 million acres in California, Oregon, and Washington. The fires destroyed over 10,000 structures, including homes and businesses. The 2019-2020 bushfire season in Australia burned over 46 million acres and destroyed over 5,900 buildings.

- **Air Quality:**

Wildfires can create a lot of smoke and ash, which can reduce air quality and make it difficult to breathe. In 2020, smoke from the wildfires on the west coast of the United States caused air quality to reach hazardous levels in some areas. During the 2019-2020 bushfire season in Australia, the city of Canberra had the worst air quality in the world due to the smoke from the fires.

2. Long-Term Effects

• Soil Erosion:

After a wildfire, the loss of vegetation can leave the soil exposed to erosion. This can cause sediment to wash into streams and rivers, which can harm aquatic life and disrupt ecosystems. For example, in 2016, a wildfire in Fort McMurray, Canada, burned over 1.4 million acres and caused significant soil erosion. The sediment runoff from the fire damaged fish habitats and threatened the health of local rivers and lakes.

• Habitat Loss:

Wildfires can destroy the habitats of many different species of wildlife and can even lead to the extinction of some species. The 2019-2020 bushfire season in Australia is estimated to have killed over 3 billion animals, including mammals, birds, and reptiles. In the United States, wildfires have threatened the habitat of endangered species like the California condor and the red-cockaded woodpecker.

- **Climate Change:**

Wildfires can contribute to climate change by releasing carbon dioxide and other greenhouse gases into the atmosphere. In 2020, the wildfires in California alone released an estimated 91 million metric tons of carbon dioxide into the atmosphere. This is equivalent to the emissions from 19 million cars in a year. Globally, wildfires are estimated to release between 2 and 9 gigatons of carbon dioxide into the atmosphere each year.

3. Human Health

• Smoke Exposure:

Wildfires can create a lot of smoke, which can contain harmful chemicals and particles that can be dangerous to breathe. In 2020, smoke from the wildfires on the west coast of the United States caused respiratory problems and other health issues for many people. During the 2019-2020 bushfire season in Australia, hospitals reported an increase in patients with respiratory issues due to the smoke.

• Mental Health:

Wildfires can also have a significant impact on people's mental health, especially for those who have lost their homes or loved ones. A survey of residents affected by the 2017 wildfires in California found that 43% reported experiencing symptoms of depression or anxiety. A study of people affected by the 2009 wildfires in Victoria, Australia, found that over 20% experienced symptoms of post-traumatic stress disorder (PTSD).

Overall, wildfires can have devastating effects on the environment, wildlife, and people. It's important to understand these effects and work to prevent and manage wildfires to protect the environment and the people who live in it.

CHAPTER 4:

The Connection Between Wildfires and Public Health

Wildfires can have a significant impact on public health, both during and after the fire. In addition to the direct health risks posed by the fire itself, such as smoke inhalation and burns, wildfires can also have indirect effects that can impact the health of individuals in the surrounding area.

During a wildfire, the smoke produced by the fire can be a significant health risk. Smoke inhalation can irritate the eyes, nose, and throat and can exacerbate existing respiratory conditions such as asthma or chronic obstructive pulmonary disease (COPD). In some cases, exposure to wildfire smoke can also cause more serious health problems such as heart attacks and stroke.

After a wildfire, there can be additional health risks posed by the smoke, as well as by the destruction of buildings and infrastructure. Burned materials such as asbestos, lead, and other hazardous materials can be released into the air, water, and soil, posing a significant risk to public health. In addition, the destruction of homes and other buildings can lead to the release of mold and other toxins that can cause respiratory problems.

Beyond the direct health risks posed by wildfires, there can also be indirect effects on public health. Wildfires can lead to the displacement of individuals and can disrupt access to healthcare, clean water, and other vital resources. In addition, the economic impact of wildfires can lead to increased stress and mental health problems in affected communities.

As we work to prevent and mitigate the impact of wildfires, it is important to consider the potential public health risks associated with these events. This includes taking steps to reduce smoke exposure, such as using air filters and staying indoors during periods of high smoke. It also means taking steps to minimize the release of hazardous materials during and after wildfires and providing support to affected communities to help them recover from the impact of these events. By considering the connection between wildfires and public health, we can work to minimize the impact of these events on individuals and communities.

28

CHAPTER 5:

Preventing Wildfires

While wildfires can be difficult to predict and control, there are steps we can take to prevent them from happening or minimize their impact.

1. Education and Awareness

- **Teach Fire Safety:**

It's important to teach children and adults about fire safety, including the dangers of playing with fire, leaving campfires unattended, and smoking in areas prone to wildfires.

Fires caused by people are a major source of wildfires. In fact, according to the National Park Service, up to 90% of wildfires in the United States are caused by human activity. This means that we all have a responsibility to learn about fire safety and practice responsible behavior to prevent wildfires.

- **Spread Awareness:**

Educate others about the risks of wildfires and the importance of fire prevention measures. This includes encouraging others to report any signs of wildfire quickly and to follow any fire safety regulations in their area.

In addition to practicing responsible behavior ourselves, it's important to spread awareness about wildfire risks and fire prevention measures to others. By educating others about the risks and importance of fire prevention, we can work together to prevent wildfires.

2. Fire Prevention Measures

- **Firebreaks:**

Firebreaks are areas where natural or man-made barriers are created to stop the spread of wildfires. These can include cleared areas, roads, and rivers.

Firebreaks can be an effective way to prevent wildfires from spreading. In some cases, firefighters will create a firebreak by digging a trench or using heavy machinery to clear away vegetation. In other cases, natural firebreaks like rivers or rocky outcroppings can help slow or stop the spread of wildfire.

- **Controlled Burns:**

Controlled burns are prescribed fires set by trained professionals to reduce fuel loads and prevent the buildup of dead plant material that can fuel wildfires.

Controlled burns are an important tool in preventing wildfires. By burning off excess fuel, controlled burns can reduce the risk of large, catastrophic wildfires. In addition, controlled burns can help maintain healthy ecosystems by promoting new growth and reducing the buildup of dead plant material.

- **Landscaping:**

Landscaping can also play a role in fire prevention by reducing the number of flammable materials near homes and other structures. This can include creating defensible space, which is a buffer zone around a home or structure that is clear of flammable materials.

Landscaping can be an important way to prevent wildfires from spreading to homes and other structures. By creating defensible space around a home or other structure, homeowners can reduce the risk of their property being damaged or destroyed by a wildfire.

3. Technology and Research

- **Early Detection:**

Early detection systems, such as cameras and sensors, can help detect wildfires before they become too large and difficult to control.

Early detection is an important part of preventing wildfires from becoming large, catastrophic events. By detecting wildfires early, firefighters can respond quickly and work to contain the fire before it spreads too far.

- **Weather Monitoring:**

Weather monitoring can also play a role in wildfire prevention by providing information on hot, dry, and windy conditions that increase the risk of wildfire.

Weather is a major factor in wildfire risk. Hot, dry, and windy conditions can make wildfires more likely to occur and more difficult to control. By monitoring weather conditions, fire agencies can be better prepared to respond to wildfires.

- **Research and Development:**

Ongoing research and development of new technologies and strategies for preventing wildfires can also help reduce the risks associated with wildfires.

Research and development are important tools in preventing wildfires. By continually exploring new technologies and strategies for preventing wildfires, we can work to reduce the risks associated with these destructive events. For example, researchers are exploring the use of drones to monitor and map wildfires, which can help firefighters more accurately target their efforts and better understand the spread of the fire.

Another area of research is the development of new firefighting equipment and techniques. For example, some firefighters are now using specialized foam to create a barrier around homes and other structures to prevent wildfires from reaching them.

In addition, researchers are working to better understand the behavior of wildfires, including how they spread and the environmental factors that contribute to their severity. This information can help inform fire prevention strategies and improve our ability to respond to wildfires.

Overall, preventing wildfires requires a combination of education, awareness, and the use of technology and research. By working together to prevent wildfires, we can help protect our communities, homes, and natural landscapes from these destructive events.

CHAPTER 6:

Fighting Wildfires

Fighting wildfires is a complex and challenging task that requires the coordination of multiple agencies and the use of specialized equipment and tactics. When a wildfire breaks out, the first responders on the scene are usually local firefighters who are trained to contain and extinguish the fire.

1. Fire Lines

One of the most common tactics used by firefighters is the creation of fire lines, which are cleared strips of land that act as a barrier between the wildfire and the surrounding area. Firefighters use hand tools and heavy equipment, such as bulldozers and excavators, to clear vegetation and other debris from the fire line. They may also use controlled burns, which involve intentionally setting small fires to burn up the fuel in the path of the wildfire.

Fire lines are essential in fighting wildfires, as they create a physical barrier that helps to prevent the fire from spreading. Firefighters use a variety of tools to create fire lines, including chainsaws, shovels, and axes. They may also use specialized equipment, such as masticators, which are machines that can quickly clear brush and other vegetation from an area.

2. Aerial Firefighting

Aerial firefighting is another important tool used to combat wildfires. Helicopters and airplanes can drop water or fire retardant chemicals on the flames, helping to slow the spread of the fire and give firefighters on the ground a chance to gain control.

There are several types of aircraft used in aerial firefighting, including fixed-wing aircraft and helicopters. Fixed-wing aircraft are typically used for dropping large amounts of water or fire retardant on the fire, while helicopters are often used for more precise drops in difficult-to-reach areas.

3. Controlled Burns

In some cases, firefighters may use controlled burns to combat wildfires. Controlled burns involve intentionally setting small fires to burn up the fuel in the path of the wildfire. This can help to slow the spread of the fire and make it easier for firefighters to contain it.

Controlled burns are carefully planned and executed, with firefighters taking into account factors such as wind speed, humidity, and temperature to ensure that the burn remains under control. They may also use specialized equipment, such as drip torches or flares, to start and control the burn.

4.   Technology   in   Wildfire Fighting

In recent years, technology has played an increasingly important role in firefighting efforts. For example, drones can be used to provide real-time images of the fire, helping firefighters to better understand its behavior and identify areas of concern. Firefighters also use GPS mapping technology to track the location of the fire and monitor its progress.

Another important technological development is the use of fire-retardant gels, which can be applied to structures to help prevent them from catching fire. Firefighters may also use specialized foam to create a barrier around homes and other structures to prevent wildfires from reaching them.

5. Risks and Challenges

Despite the efforts of firefighters, wildfires can still be extremely difficult to control, particularly when weather conditions are unfavorable. In some cases, wildfires may burn for weeks or even months before they are finally contained.

In addition to the physical challenges of fighting wildfires, firefighters also face significant risks to their safety. Wildfires can produce intense heat, smoke, and flames, making it difficult for firefighters to see and breathe. In addition, falling trees, rocks, and other debris can pose a danger to firefighters on the ground.

Despite these challenges, firefighters continue to work tirelessly to protect communities and natural landscapes from the devastating effects of wildfires. Through their bravery and dedication, they serve as a reminder of the importance of preparedness, prevention, and cooperation in the fight against wildfires.

CHAPTER 7:

The Role of Technology in Fighting Wildfires

Technology has become an essential tool in the fight against wildfires. New advances in technology have made it possible for firefighters and other first responders to better predict and prevent wildfires, as well as to more effectively manage and extinguish them once they occur.

One of the most important technological advancements in wildfire prevention is the use of satellite imagery and other remote sensing technologies. These tools allow scientists and fire managers to monitor weather patterns, vegetation moisture levels, and other key indicators of wildfire risk. This information can then be used to create early warning systems and to develop strategies for managing wildfire outbreaks before they become catastrophic.

Another key area of technological development in the fight against wildfires is in the realm of firefighting equipment and gear. Firefighters today have access to a wide range of specialized tools and equipment that can help them more effectively battle wildfires. This can include everything from specialized firefighting suits and helmets to advanced fire suppression systems, such as fire-retardant gels and foams.

In addition to technology that is directly related to firefighting, there are also a number of technology-driven initiatives underway to promote wildfire prevention and education. For example, there are now mobile apps available that provide real-time information on wildfire risks and conditions. These apps can also provide users with information on how to stay safe during a wildfire, as well as tips on how to prevent fires from occurring in the first place.

While technology has certainly played an important role in the fight against wildfires, it is important to remember that it is only one piece of the puzzle. Effective wildfire management still relies heavily on the expertise and experience of trained firefighters and other first responders. Nevertheless, the continued development of new technologies is likely to play an increasingly important role in mitigating the impact of wildfires in the years to come.

46

CHAPTER 8:

After the Wildfire

After a wildfire has been extinguished, the effects of the fire can still be felt for weeks, months, and even years afterward. The aftermath of a wildfire can be devastating, with homes destroyed, wildlife habitats disrupted, and entire landscapes transformed.

1. Assessing the Damage

After a wildfire has been put out, the first step is to assess the damage. This involves evaluating the extent of the fire and its impact on homes, businesses, and natural resources. This process is often carried out by teams of experts, including firefighters, land managers, and environmental scientists.

During this assessment phase, teams may use a variety of tools and techniques to evaluate the damage caused by the fire. For example, they may use drones to survey the area from above, or they may conduct ground surveys to evaluate the health of vegetation and other natural resources.

2. Restoring the Landscape

One of the most important steps in the aftermath of a wildfire is restoring the landscape. This involves replanting vegetation, removing dead trees and other debris, and implementing erosion control measures to prevent soil erosion and protect water quality.

Restoration efforts may be carried out by a variety of organizations, including federal and state agencies, nonprofit organizations, and local communities. In many cases, these efforts involve a combination of manual labor and advanced technologies, such as drones and other remote-sensing equipment.

3. Supporting Wildlife

Wildfires can have a profound impact on wildlife habitats, often destroying homes and habitats for animals. After a wildfire, it's important to provide support for wildlife to help them recover and rebuild their populations.

This may involve creating new habitats, providing food and water sources, and implementing other measures to support wildlife populations. In some cases, wildlife may need to be relocated to new areas to ensure their survival.

4. Supporting Communities

The aftermath of a wildfire can be a difficult time for communities that have been impacted by the fire. Homes and businesses may have been destroyed, and individuals and families may have lost their homes and possessions.

In order to support affected communities, a variety of organizations may offer resources and services such as counseling, financial assistance, and access to temporary housing. Communities may also come together to support each other through fundraising efforts and volunteer work.

5. Preventing Future Wildfires

Perhaps the most important step in the aftermath of a wildfire is taking steps to prevent future wildfires. This involves a combination of preparedness measures, such as creating defensible spaces around homes and businesses, and prevention efforts, such as enforcing fire restrictions and educating the public about fire safety.

Preventing future wildfires also involves addressing underlying issues that contribute to the risk of wildfires, such as climate change and drought conditions. By taking proactive steps to prevent future wildfires, communities can help to protect their homes, businesses, and natural resources from future disasters.

The aftermath of a wildfire can be a difficult and challenging time, but with the right tools and resources, communities can come together to recover and rebuild. Through a combination of restoration efforts, wildlife support, community support, and prevention measures, we can work to minimize the impact of wildfires and protect our homes, businesses, and natural resources for generations to come.

CHAPTER 9:

The Role of Animals in Ecosystem Recovery

Wildfires can have a significant impact on the ecosystems in which they occur. In addition to the destruction of trees and other vegetation, wildfires can also have a profound effect on the animals that live in affected areas. However, even in the aftermath of a devastating wildfire, there is hope for recovery, thanks in part to the important role that animals play in ecosystem restoration.

One of the most important ways that animals contribute to ecosystem recovery is by helping to disperse seeds and nutrients. Animals such as birds and mammals can eat fruits and other plant material and then deposit seeds and nutrients throughout the environment as they travel. This can help to jumpstart the growth of new vegetation in areas that have been burned by wildfire.

In addition to seed dispersal, animals can also play a crucial role in controlling invasive species. In the aftermath of a wildfire, invasive plant species can often take hold and compete with native plants for resources. However, animals such as deer and rabbits can help to control these invasions by grazing on the invasive plants and allowing native species to thrive.

Another way that animals contribute to ecosystem recovery is through nutrient cycling. As animals eat and excrete, they help to move nutrients through the ecosystem, facilitating the growth of new vegetation and supporting the recovery of the ecosystem as a whole.

While the role of animals in ecosystem recovery is important, it is important to note that not all animals are equally beneficial. Some animals, such as wild pigs, can actually cause damage to ecosystems by rooting up plants and disrupting the soil. However, many other animals, such as birds, mammals, and insects, play a vital role in supporting the recovery of ecosystems affected by wildfires.

As we work to prevent and mitigate the impact of wildfires, it is important to consider the role that animals play in ecosystem recovery. By protecting and preserving the habitats of these important animals, we can support the restoration of ecosystems in the aftermath of devastating wildfires.

CHAPTER 10:

Preserving Our National Parks

National parks are natural treasures that are home to a diverse range of plants, animals, and ecosystems. Unfortunately, wildfires can pose a significant threat to these areas and can have a lasting impact on the park's flora and fauna. As a result, it is important to take steps to prevent wildfires from occurring in our national parks and to work to protect these areas from the devastating impact of these events.

One of the key ways to prevent wildfires in national parks is through education and awareness. Visitors to these areas should be informed of the risks associated with wildfires and should be provided with information on how to prevent them. This can include information on proper campfire procedures, as well as information on how to safely dispose of cigarettes and other fire hazards.

In addition to prevention efforts, it is also important to develop effective strategies for managing wildfires when they do occur. This can include techniques such as prescribed burns, which can help to reduce the amount of fuel available for future wildfires and can also promote the growth of new vegetation. Other strategies can include creating firebreaks, which are areas that have been cleared of vegetation in order to prevent the spread of fires.

Beyond prevention and management, there are also efforts underway to restore areas of national parks that have been impacted by wildfires. This can include replanting native vegetation, restoring habitats, and working to mitigate erosion and other environmental impacts that can result from wildfires.

Preserving our national parks is critical not only for the plants and animals that call these areas home but also for future generations of Americans who will have the opportunity to experience the beauty and wonder of these areas. By taking steps to prevent wildfires and by working to protect and restore these areas when they are impacted by these events, we can help to ensure that our national parks remain healthy and vibrant for years to come.

CHAPTER 11:

The Future of Wildfires

As the effects of climate change continue to be felt around the world, there is growing concern about the future of wildfires. Scientists predict that wildfires will become more frequent, larger, and more intense in many parts of the world in the coming decades.

One factor contributing to this trend is the increasing frequency and severity of droughts. Droughts leave forests and other vegetation dry and susceptible to fire and are expected to become more common in many areas due to climate change. As temperatures rise, the risk of wildfires is also expected to increase, as hot, dry conditions create ideal conditions for fires to start and spread.

In addition to climate change, human activities also contribute to the risk of wildfires. For example, the expansion of housing into wildland areas has increased the risk of wildfires, as more people live in areas that are susceptible to fire. Additionally, the practice of suppressing wildfires for many decades has resulted in an accumulation of vegetation that can fuel large, intense fires when they do occur.

Despite the challenges posed by climate change and other factors, there are many efforts underway to prevent and mitigate the impacts of wildfires. These include:

- Increasing public awareness about the risks of wildfires and the steps that individuals can take to reduce their risk of starting or spreading fires.
- Improving firefighting techniques and technology, such as using drones and other advanced tools to detect and fight fires more effectively.
- Implementing controlled burns and other techniques to reduce the buildup of fuel that can make fires more intense.
- Working with communities to create fire-resistant landscapes and homes, using fire-resistant materials and other techniques to reduce the risk of wildfire damage.
- Investing in research to better understand the factors that contribute to wildfires and how they can be prevented or mitigated.

Ultimately, the future of wildfires will depend on the actions that we take in the coming years and decades. By working together to address the root causes of wildfires, we can help to reduce the risk of devastating fires and ensure that our communities and natural landscapes are protected for generations to come.

CHAPTER 12:

Being Fire-Smart at Home

You can play an important role in preventing wildfires by practicing fire safety at home. While wildfires may seem like a distant threat, it's important to remember that many wildfires start from small fires in and around homes. By being fire-smart at home, you can help prevent fires from starting in your own community.

1. Tips for Fire-Smart Behavior at Home

There are several steps you can take to practice fire-smart behavior at home. Here are a few tips:

- **Avoid the use of matches or lighters:**

Matches and lighters can be dangerous. You should never play with matches or lighters and always report any found to an adult.

- **Be cautious with candles and other open flames:**

Candles and other open flames can easily ignite nearby objects. You should never leave candles burning unattended, keep candles away from flammable materials, and use flameless candles instead when possible.

- **Practice kitchen safety:**

Many home fires start in the kitchen. You should always keep a close eye on cooking food, never leave the stove or oven unattended, and keep flammable materials away from the stove.

2. Keep a Fire-Safety Checklist

Creating a fire-safety checklist is a great way to ensure that you are taking all necessary precautions to prevent fires at home. You can include things like checking smoke detectors regularly, creating a family evacuation plan, and storing flammable materials safely.

3. Educate Yourself and Others

Education is key to preventing fires at home. You should learn as much as you can about fire safety and share this information with your family and friends. This can include information about fire prevention techniques, how to safely use campfires and grills, and how to report fires and other hazards.

4. Take Action

Finally, it's important to take action to prevent fires at home. If you see something that could potentially start a fire, speak up and report it to an adult. By being proactive and responsible, you can help keep your community safe from wildfires.

CHAPTER 13:

Spreading Awareness

One of the most important things you can do to prevent wildfires is to spread awareness. By educating yourself and others about the dangers of wildfires and how to prevent them, you can help protect your community and the environment.

1. Educate Yourself

The first step in spreading awareness is to educate yourself about wildfires. You can learn about the causes of wildfires, how they spread, and the impact they can have on the environment and communities. You can also learn about fire safety and prevention techniques that can be used at home, in the wilderness, and in public places.

2. Share Your Knowledge

Once you have educated yourself about wildfires, you can share your knowledge with others. You can start by talking to your family and friends about the importance of fire safety and prevention. You can also share information on social media or through community newsletters and other outlets.

3. Get Involved

Another way to spread awareness is to get involved in community organizations and events that focus on wildfire prevention. You can volunteer with organizations that work to prevent and mitigate the impact of wildfires, such as fire departments, conservation groups, or local environmental organizations.

4. Organize Community Events

Organizing community events is another great way to spread awareness about wildfires. You can plan events such as town hall meetings, educational seminars, or workshops that focus on fire prevention techniques and wildfire safety. You can also organize fundraising events to support local wildfire prevention efforts.

5. Create Educational Materials

Creating educational materials is another effective way to spread awareness about wildfires. You can create flyers, brochures, or posters that provide information about fire safety and prevention techniques. You can also create educational videos or podcasts that can be shared on social media or other platforms.

6. Be a Role Model

Finally, the most important way to spread awareness about wildfires is to be a role model. By practicing fire-smart behavior at home and in public, you can set an example for others to follow. You can also encourage your family and friends to adopt fire-smart behaviors and lead by example in your community. Together, we can all work to prevent wildfires and protect our communities and the environment.

CHAPTER 14:

Volunteering and Supporting Fire Prevention Efforts

Volunteering and supporting fire prevention efforts are critical ways you can make a difference in reducing the risk and impact of wildfires in your community.

1. Volunteer Opportunities

There are many opportunities to volunteer and support fire prevention efforts. Here are a few examples:

- Join a local fire department or emergency response team. These organizations rely heavily on volunteers and provide critical support during wildfires.
- Volunteer with a local conservation group. These groups often work on land management and restoration projects that can help reduce the risk of wildfires.
- Participate in a community-wide cleanup event. Removing debris, dead vegetation, and other materials can help reduce the risk of wildfires in your area.
- Attend a fire prevention training course. These courses teach you about fire behavior, fire prevention, and how to respond in the event of a wildfire.

2. Supporting Fire Prevention Efforts

Even if you can't volunteer, there are still ways you can support fire prevention efforts. Here are a few examples:

- Donate to local fire departments or emergency response teams. These organizations rely on funding to maintain equipment and training.
- Support local conservation groups or organizations that work to prevent wildfires. Donations can be used for land management, restoration projects, or outreach and education efforts.
- Participate in local community planning and development processes. Ensuring that new construction follows fire-resistant building codes and guidelines can help reduce the risk of wildfires.

- Spread awareness about fire prevention efforts in your community. Share information about fire-smart behavior, volunteer opportunities, and organizations that support wildfire prevention.

3. Benefits of Volunteering and Supporting Fire Prevention Efforts

Volunteering and supporting fire prevention efforts have many benefits. Not only do they help reduce the risk and impact of wildfires, but they also provide opportunities to learn new skills, meet new people, and give back to your community. Additionally, supporting these efforts can help build stronger, more resilient communities that are better equipped to respond to natural disasters.

By volunteering and supporting fire prevention efforts, you can make a significant impact in reducing the risk and impact of wildfires in your community. Whether you join a local fire department or simply spread awareness about fire prevention efforts, every action you take can help protect your community and the environment.

CHAPTER 15:

Small Actions, Big Impact

Small actions can have a big impact when it comes to preventing wildfires. While it may seem like a daunting task to stop something as large and destructive as a wildfire, there are many simple steps that individuals can take to reduce the risk of fires starting in the first place.

One of the easiest ways to prevent wildfires is to be careful with fire. This means making sure that campfires and other open flames are properly contained and extinguished and never leaving them unattended. It also means being careful with cigarettes and other smoking materials and properly disposing of them in designated receptacles.

Another important way to prevent wildfires is to be mindful of dry and flammable materials. This can include things like dead leaves, branches, and grasses, which can easily ignite and spread a fire. By taking simple steps like raking leaves and clearing brush, individuals can help reduce the risk of fires starting in their communities.

Another important step in preventing wildfires is to be aware of local fire regulations and to follow them closely. This may mean following rules regarding outdoor burning, using fireworks, and other activities that can increase the risk of fires.

In addition to these steps, individuals can also help prevent wildfires by supporting fire prevention efforts in their communities. This can include volunteering with local fire departments, supporting initiatives aimed at promoting wildfire prevention and education and advocating for policies that prioritize wildfire prevention and management.

Finally, it's important to remember that preventing wildfires is everyone's responsibility. By taking small actions and making smart choices, individuals can play a critical role in reducing the risk of wildfires and protecting their communities from the devastating effects of these natural disasters.

CONCLUSION

In conclusion, wildfires are a natural phenomenon that have been around for millions of years, but their impact has been amplified in recent years due to human activities such as climate change, deforestation, and urbanization. However, there are steps we can take to reduce the risk of wildfires and protect ourselves and our communities.

We have learned that wildfires have a significant impact on the environment, economy, and public health. They destroy homes and habitats, contribute to air pollution and climate change, and cause immense economic losses. But we have also learned that by taking action to prevent wildfires and manage them effectively, we can reduce their impact and even restore damaged ecosystems.

As individuals, we can play a critical role in preventing wildfires by being fire-smart, spreading awareness, volunteering, and supporting fire prevention efforts. We can make a difference by being mindful of dry and flammable materials, following fire regulations, supporting fire prevention initiatives, and making smart choices when it comes to fire safety.

The future of wildfires is uncertain, but with continued effort and dedication, we can work towards reducing the risk of wildfires and protecting our planet. It is our responsibility to take action and work towards a safer and more sustainable future.

Remember, small actions can have a big impact. By working together and taking small steps toward wildfire prevention, we can make a big difference and protect our communities and our planet for generations to come.